STAR WARS™
THE CLONE WARS™

Score by KEVIN KINER

Original Star Wars Themes and Score by JOHN WILLIAMS

Arranged by Carol Tornquist

Alfred Publishing Co., Inc.
16320 Roscoe Blvd., Suite 100
P.O. Box 10003
Van Nuys, CA 91410-0003
alfred.com

ISBN-10: 0-7390-5876-2
ISBN-13: 978-0-7390-5876-3

T0052757

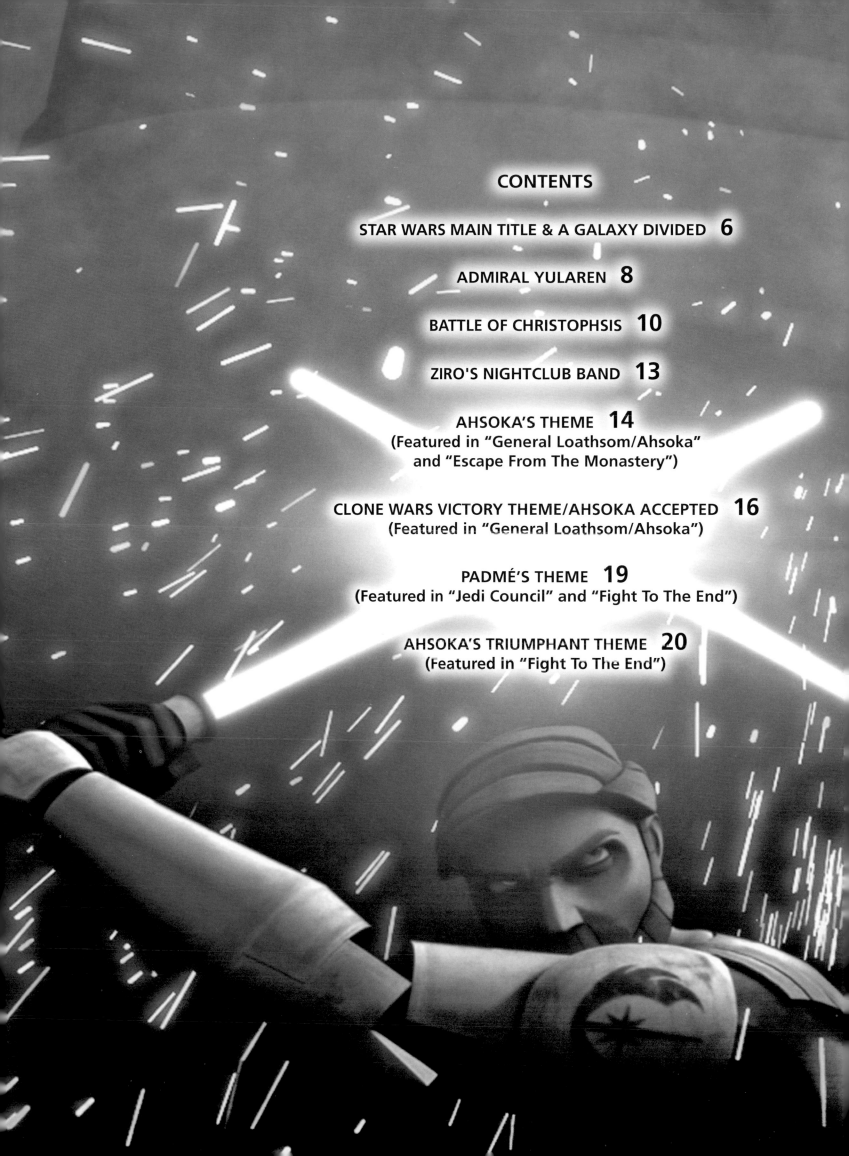

CONTENTS

STAR WARS takes on a dazzling new look in the first-ever animated feature from Lucasfilm Animation - **STAR WARS: THE CLONE WARS**. As the Clone Wars sweep through the galaxy, the heroic Jedi Knights struggle to maintain order and restore peace. More and more systems are falling prey to the forces of the dark side as the Galactic Republic slips further and further under the sway of the Separatists and their never-ending droid army. Anakin Skywalker and his Padawan learner Ahsoka Tano find themselves on a mission with far-reaching consequences, one that brings them face-to-face with crime lord Jabba the Hutt. But Count Dooku and his sinister agents, including the nefarious Asajj Ventress, will stop at nothing to ensure that Anakin and Ahsoka fail at their quest. Meanwhile, on the front lines of the Clone Wars, Obi-Wan Kenobi and Master Yoda lead the massive clone army in a valiant effort to resist the forces of the dark side ...

STAR WARS MAIN TITLE & A GALAXY DIVIDED

Star Wars Main Title by **JOHN WILLIAMS**
A Galaxy Divided by Kevin Kiner
Arranged by Carol Tornquist

ADMIRAL YULAREN

By Kevin Kiner
Arranged by Carol Tornquist

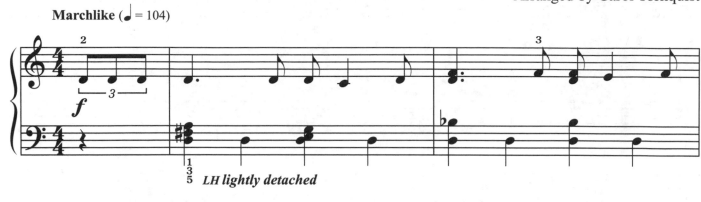

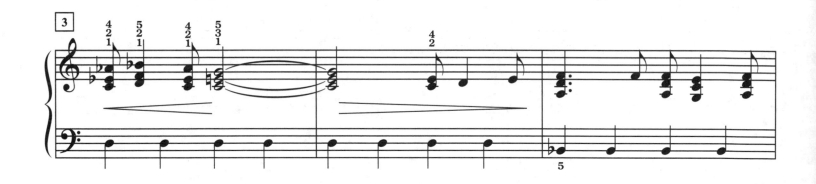

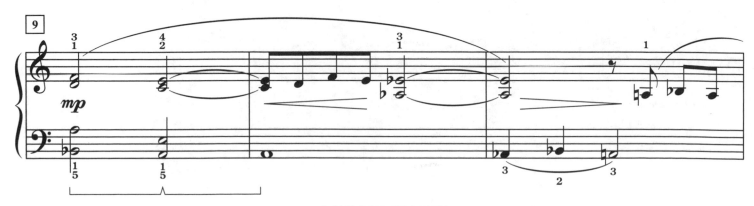

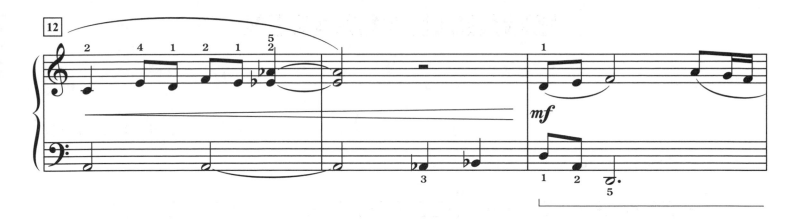

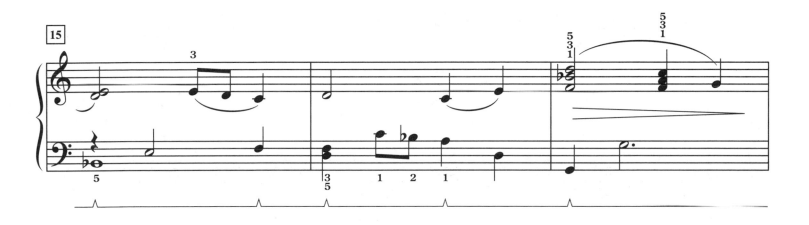

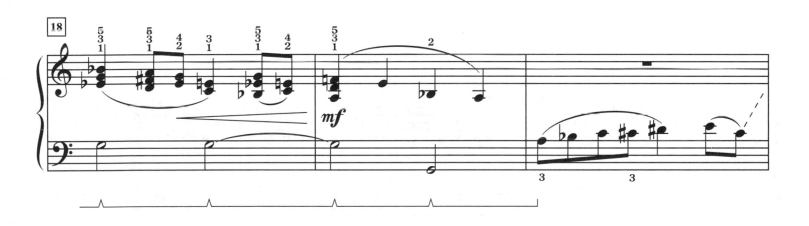

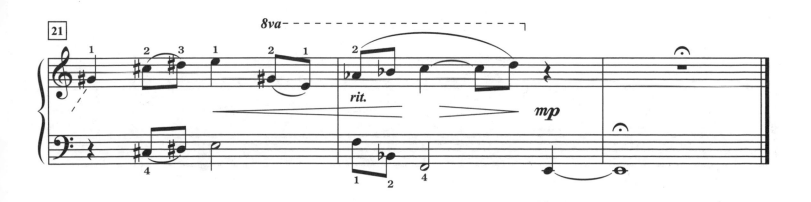

BATTLE OF CHRISTOPHSIS

By Kevin Kiner
Arranged by Carol Tornquist

Moderately, rhythmic (♩ = 96)

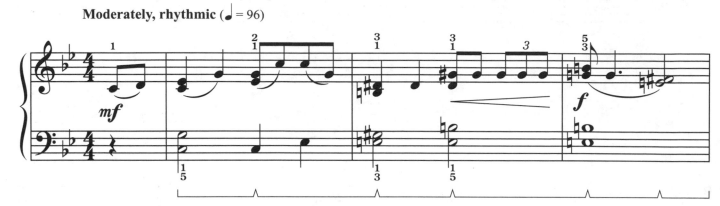

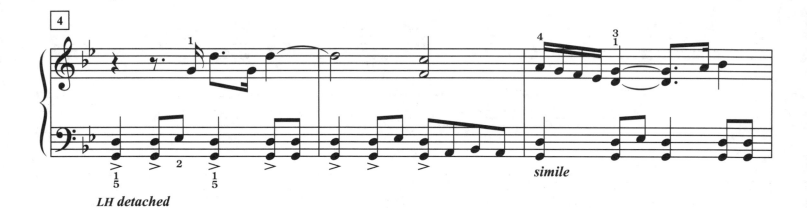

LH detached

LH lightly detached

ZIRO'S NIGHTCLUB BAND

By Kevin Kiner
Arranged by Carol Tornquist

AHSOKA'S THEME

(Featured in "General Loathsom/Ahsoka" and "Escape From The Monastery")

By Kevin Kiner
Arranged by Carol Tornquist

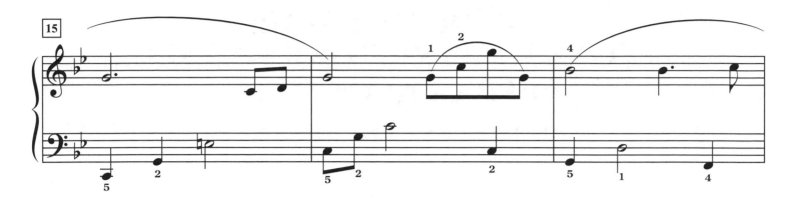

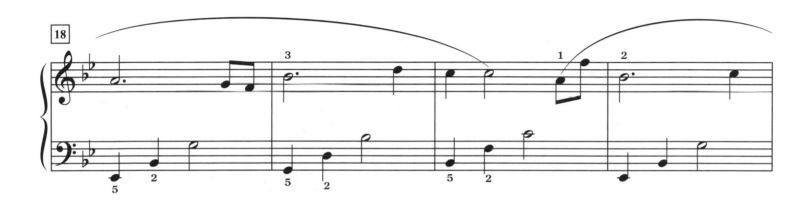

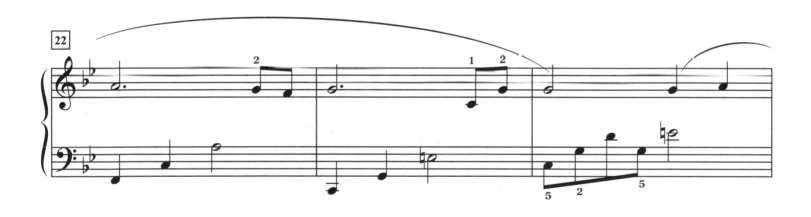

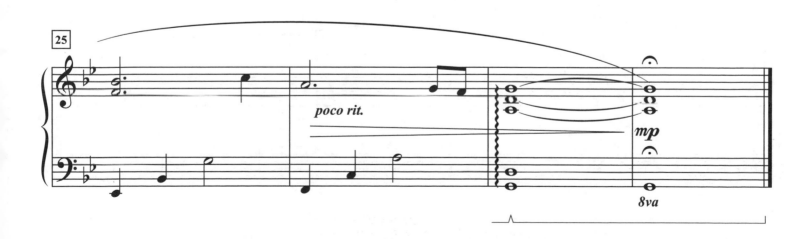

CLONE WARS VICTORY THEME/ AHSOKA ACCEPTED

(Featured in "General Loathsom/Ahsoka")

By Kevin Kiner
Arranged by Carol Tornquist

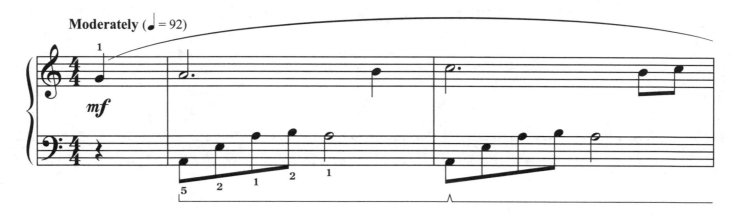

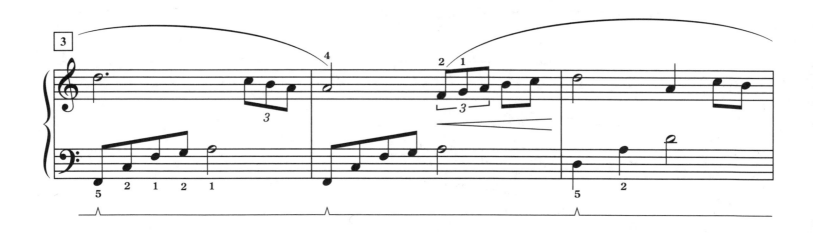

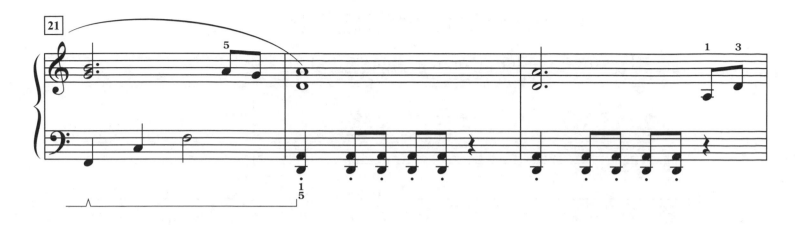

simile

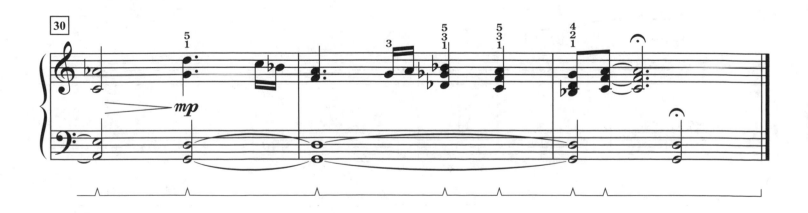

mp

PADMÉ'S THEME

(Featured in "Jedi Council" and "Fight To The End")

By Kevin Kiner
Arranged by Carol Tornquist

AHSOKA'S TRIUMPHANT THEME

(Featured in "Fight To The End")

By Kevin Kiner
Arranged by Carol Tornquist

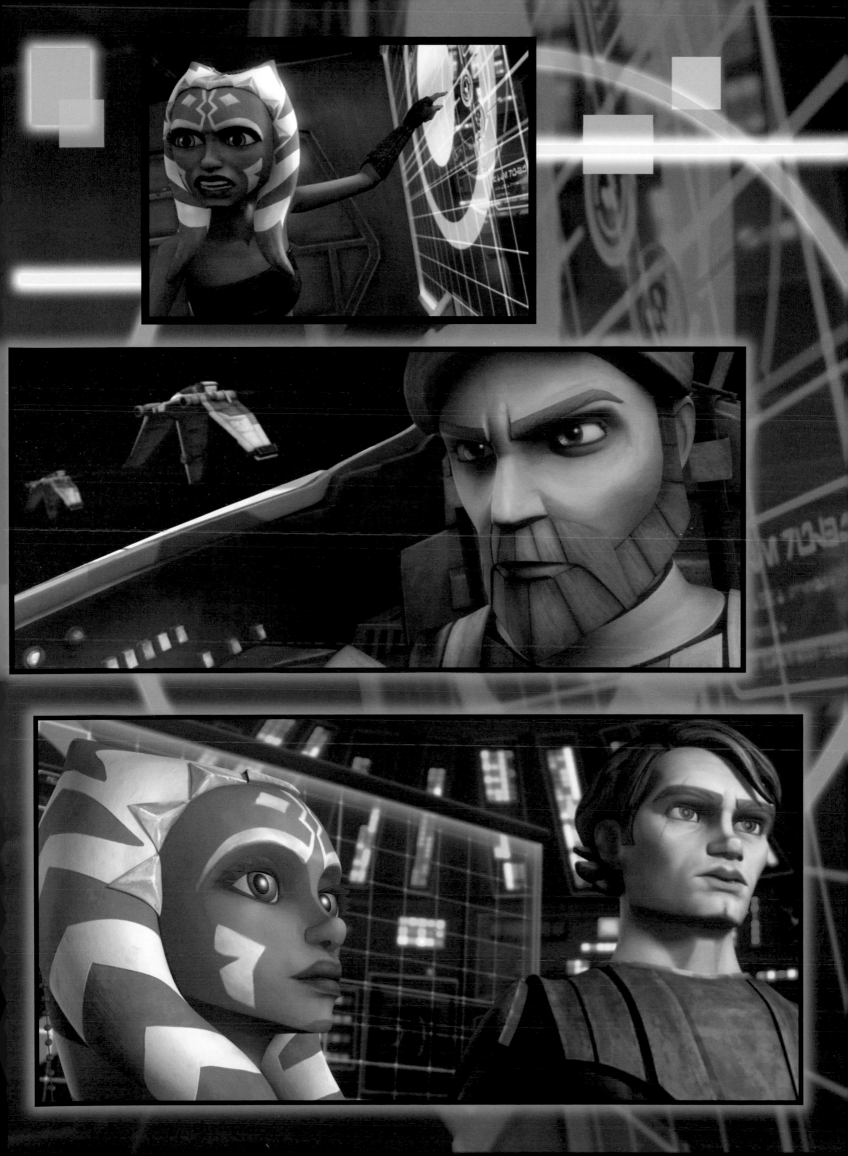